Jean Khoury

Small Catechism on *Lectio Divina*

100 questions and answers to learn how to listen and put into practice a Word every day.

www.schoolofmary.org

Revised by Francesca Crocker

Cover Artwork: The Annunciation by Françoise Faugeras

I want to thank Anna Maria Cattaneo for her intelligent and decisive contribution to the creation of this book. Without her tireless collaboration, the book would not have come to fruition.

Contents

Preface _____ 5

Introduction _____ 7

    1- The Purpose Of This Book _____ 9

    2- Definition, Necessity, And Benefits Of *Lectio Divina* _____ 9

Part I - The Starting Point Of *Lectio Divina* _____ 13

    1 - The Eternal Word Becomes Words That Are Spirit And Life _____ 15

    2 - Through The Readings Of The Mass, Christ Offers Us A Word Every Day _____ 17

    3 - Mary Is Our Model In Receiving The Word ____ 19

    4 - Nourishing Oneself With The Word: Its Necessity, Stages, And Our Responsibility _____ 21

    5- The Determination To Dedicate Time; The Prayer To Find It _____ 25

Part II- The Practice Of *Lectio Divina* _____ 29

   1- How To Practise *Lectio Divina* _____ 32

   2- Let Us Delve Deeper Into *Lectio Divina* _____ 39

Part III – The Effort Of *Lectio Divina* And The Fruits That Come From It _____ 53

   1- Entering Through The Narrow Door _____ 55

   2- The Temptations To Escape _____ 60

   3- Fruits Of *Lectio* _____ 61

   4- Lectio And The Prayer Of The Heart _____ 64

5. The Growth Of Spiritual Life _____ 67

Conclusion _____ 71

Preface

It has been an immense grace to be led by God, through a friend, to practise what we might today call a *Lectio Divina* based on the daily readings of the Mass. This has been the most powerful force for transformation in my spiritual life. As Enzo Bianchi once said, *"Scripture has returned from exile."* He was referring to the exile imposed by the Counter-Reformation. The publication of the new *Lectionary* of the Roman Latin Rite in December 1969 played a crucial role in this silent revolution.

Today, more than ever, we have unprecedented access to Scripture through excellent translations, study Bibles, scholarly publications, and courses. Truly, we are living in a golden age. This abundance allows us to encounter the Lord more profoundly during the Mass, particularly in the Proclamation of the Word. Indeed, He comes to speak to each one of us in the depths of our hearts, offering us the *daily bread* He has prepared.

Sitting at His feet each day, listening with a heart like Mary's, has become a widespread habit among the People of God—a practice long treasured by monastic tradition.

I have had the privilege of teaching *Lectio Divina* since 1992 and have never stopped doing so. In 1999, as a result of this teaching, a young woman approached me after one of my lessons and asked if I had *"something written on Lectio."* That simple question marked the beginning of what would become *Lectio Divina at the School of Mary*, later published in multiple languages.

I continued teaching, and in 2004–2005, while in Italy, I became aware of a significant challenge in the practice of *Lectio Divina*: the difficulty of moving from the general light given by Jesus to a more specific, personal one. I felt the need to address this issue in writing, which I did more recently in *Finished and Unfinished Lectio Divina* (2024).

Back to 2012: a crucial question was raised: should I rewrite my first book to present the 15 steps instead of the original 7, or should I write a completely new book? With the collaboration of Anna-Maria Cattaneo, I chose the latter. I wanted this new book to be clear, succinct, and comprehensive, designed for every parishioner. It needed to be accessible, not too long, and structured in the form of a catechism (Q&A). The result was this book. Finally, this book is now available for the English speaking reader.

The *Small Catechism on Lectio Divina* teaches, through 100 questions and answers, how to listen to the Lord Jesus, who desires to speak to us each day through the daily readings of the Mass. It is a simple and practical book for every believer. The art of listening can be summed up in two key moments:

- Listening in our hearts to the daily personal Word that the Lord gives us through the power of the Holy Spirit.
- Putting the Word into practice with the power of His strength.

This book explains in detail how to ensure that the Word takes flesh within us and bears fruit. Without this incarnation, our Christian life remains empty.

"Mary, grant us your purity in listening, your attachment to the Word of your Son, and your commitment to putting it into practice through the power of the Holy Spirit."

"This practice (Lectio Divina), if effectively promoted, will bring the Church – I am convinced – a new spiritual springtime."
— Benedict XVI

Jean Khoury
2025

Introduction

1- The Purpose of This Book

1. Why this book?
The purpose of this book is to help the reader become aware of the gift that Christ offers us every day through the readings of the Mass. It also aims to teach how to listen to and put into practice the Word that is given to us. Finally, it shows the fruits that result from it and the process of growth that the Word evokes in us, until we reach the full stature of Christ.

2. Does this book intend to teach a new method for doing *Lectio Divina*?
No, it only aims to explain with precision and clarity the inner supernatural mechanism that should be triggered in every *Lectio*, so that it becomes an effective and fruitful listening. Understanding the movement of receiving the Word and learning to verify that the Word has been received well and put into practice is essential for the success of *Lectio*, no matter which method is followed.

3. Who is this book for?
This book is for every parishioner, but also for priests, religious, and anyone who desires to learn the art of Listening and to make this sacred activity the cornerstone of their day.

2- Definition, Necessity, and Benefits of *Lectio Divina*

4. What is *Lectio Divina*?
Lectio Divina is a traditional Latin expression meaning "divine reading," or "spiritual reading," that is, reading of Sacred Scripture done "with the help of the Holy Spirit." *Lectio Divina* is the daily listening to and putting into practice a Word given to us by Christ

through the readings of the Mass. It can also be defined as a way of praying in which a daily time is consecrated to listen to the Lord, who comes every day to speak to us in our conscience through the texts of the day.

5. Is *Lectio Divina* something new?
No, it is a practice that, in its essence, has been present in the living Tradition of the Church since its origins, although its rediscovery and development are recent.

6. Why is it important to do *Lectio Divina*?
Lectio Divina is fundamental because it allows us to enter into a relationship of divine friendship with the Lord, expressing our love to Him - *"If anyone loves me, he will keep my word"* (Jn 14:23) - and allowing Him to speak in a unique and personal way to each of us, transforming us day by day into Himself. Without the Word of God, our prayer is empty and does not help us grow. The Lord reminds us of this essential truth about prayer and sums it up as follows: *"Not everyone who says to me, 'Lord, Lord,' will enter the Kingdom of Heaven"* (Mt 7:21 ff; Lk 6:46-49), but only those who keep my Word (cf. Lk 8:15).

7. Is *Lectio Divina* for everyone?
Yes, because man lives by the Word of the Lord; it is his Bread - *"Man shall not live by bread alone, but by every word that comes from the mouth of God"* (Mt 4:4) - provided he knows how to read and has a minimum of human and spiritual culture to understand the biblical text he is reading.

There are people who, for various reasons, cannot engage in *Lectio*. Illness, lack of education, or incapacity are reasons that clearly exclude the practice of *Lectio*. The Lord will indicate other paths for them to hear His voice in their conscience and do His will. However, a person who is able to do *Lectio* but does not, tempts the Lord, because they do not use the powerful means He makes available. This is an attitude of laziness and negligence.

8. A person who engages in various ecclesial activities and already prays a lot, why should they add another practice?

Because *Lectio Divina* is not an additional practice, but it realises the essence of the Gospel: listening to and putting into practice the Word of God. The Lord wants our actions to proceed from Him ("without me you can do nothing" [Jn 15:5]), from the contemplation of His will. One single act of pure love, that is, one done in God – and *Lectio* is one of these – is worth more than all the works that could be done (cf. John of the Cross, *Spiritual Canticle* B, 29,2). Now, *Lectio* connects us with the Author of our life and thus enables us to bear fruit that remains (cf. Jn 15:16) and to do God's work, not our own.

9. A person who often reads the Gospel, is that not already in some way doing *Lectio Divina*?

No, because *Lectio Divina* is not simply a reading of the Gospel or the Bible, but a specific activity that allows God to speak to us every day and transform us into Himself. There is no opposition, however, between the practice of *Lectio Divina* and any other form of engagement with Sacred Scripture, whether it be simple reading, meditation, or systematic study – in fact, they are complementary. However, since *Lectio Divina* is a nourishment, it is vital.

10. A person who goes to Mass every day, do they still need to do *Lectio Divina*?

Yes, because *Lectio*, when based on the readings of the day, helps us receive and digest the nourishment given to us in the first part of the Mass, the Table of the Word (which is the Primordial

Sacrament). *Lectio* is, in fact, like an extension, in time, of those moments – too brief – of the Liturgy of the Word.

11. What are the benefits of *Lectio Divina*?
If the Word of God is incarnated in us, we feel the wonderful and sure progress that is rapidly realised in our lives:
- Greater order in life;
- Clarity of ideas and actions that will unfold during the day;
- A stronger faith;
- A will that is freed from its slavery, becomes more solid and rooted in that of God;
- Consolation and strength, both from a daily encounter with Christ, the Living One, and from being able to understand Him as, in the silence of listening, He speaks to us and reveals His will;
- Finally, perseverance and resistance to any trial. It should also be added that one of the greatest benefits of *Lectio* is the fact that our intellect is no longer at the mercy of a thousand thoughts, but is more disciplined, because it is nourished by an intense light that illuminates it from the morning and remains throughout the day.

Part I - The Starting Point of *Lectio Divina*

1 - The Eternal Word Becomes Words that 'are Spirit and Life'

12. How does the Word become Words?
At the moment of the Annunciation, the Eternal Word (the Son, the Second Person of the Trinity) takes on a human nature, composed of body, soul (intellect and will), and spirit. From this moment, a slow and gradual process of growth takes place within the humanity of Christ, which culminates in the achievement of adulthood (cf. Lk 2:52). During this growth, in the heart and mind of Jesus, the Words are formed – Words that "are Spirit and Life" (cf. Jn 6:63) – which He will later give to us.

13. When does Jesus begin to give us His Words?
During His approximately three-and-a-half-year ministry, Jesus opens His mouth (cf. Mt 5:2) to communicate to us the ineffable gift of His Words.
The beginning of Jesus' public ministry is an unparalleled event: it is the Word that goes forth to sow His Words. The Eternal Word was hidden from our eyes and silent. Humankind could not eat the fruit of the Tree of Life. By giving us His Words, Jesus reopens the way: we can access the Tree of Life and are now able to listen to God speaking directly to us.
Therefore, the Word will travel through Palestine, sowing His Words full of life that illuminate and heal. Later, He will entrust these living Words – just as He will entrust His body and blood – to His successors, so that they may continue to spread them.
The Apostles, to whom Christ entrusted His Words, passed them on to the generations that followed, both orally and in writing. The Gospel is the written form par excellence of Christ's Words of life; it transmits them as they were preserved and meditated

upon in the hearts of those men chosen by Him and assisted by the Holy Spirit.

14. What is the characteristic of Jesus' Words?
The Words that Jesus gives us are human in their outer form, but divine in their content. They are therefore different from our words and have the power to transform them.

The Incarnation produced an absolutely unique and crucial consequence for the human intellect and will: making the Words of Jesus available, which are not only human, but full of divine sap and charged with the Holy Spirit.

15. What power do the Words of Jesus have?
The Words of Jesus have a transforming power. He invites us to experience them and to acknowledge, like Peter, that they are divine and life-giving: *"Lord, to whom shall we go? You have the words of eternal life"* (Jn 6:68). They are the daily nourishment for the reconstruction of the human being in Christ, for the growth of the new man within us. With His Words, Jesus, the Healer, heals us and communicates Divine Life to us (cf. Jn 6:63). His Words make us resemble Him. Day by day, through His Words, He comes, lives, and acts in us, making us grow *"until we all reach unity in the faith and in the knowledge of the Son of God and become mature, attaining to the whole measure of the fullness of Christ"* (Eph 4:13).

16. Are the Words of Jesus therefore true Bread?
Yes, the Words that Jesus offers us are true Bread, which nourishes our intellect and will. By assimilating it, the Word-food assimilates us and transforms us into It. Nourishing ourselves with these Words is therefore vital: *"Man shall not live by bread alone, but by every word that comes from the mouth of God"* (Mt 4:4). For this reason, the Lord invites us to ask for this food and to strive to obtain it: *"Give us today our daily bread"* (Mt 6:11).

2 - Through the Readings of the Mass, Christ Offers Us a Word Every Day

17. What does the Table of the Word consist of?

The Second Vatican Council allowed the Church to regain an awareness of the Table of the Word in the Mass and to make it more abundant and varied.

The arrangement of the readings changes depending on the different liturgical traditions, but in general, the Lectionaries share the fact that they distribute Scripture in a three-year cycle for Sunday celebrations (two years for weekday celebrations) and present at least two texts for each celebration (three on Sundays and feasts), drawn from both the Old and the New Testaments. This structure is an inheritance from the early Church. The first generations of Christians maintained the liturgical form of the Synagogue celebration, in which the entire Torah and the Prophets were read over three years, but they also added passages from the New Testament, which was gradually being formed.

Behind this choice to pair passages from the Old Testament with those from the New was an authentic contemplative experience that led them to see Jesus in both texts, thanks to the opening of the mind to the understanding of Scripture, a gift of the Spirit (cf. Lk 24:27).

Jesus accomplishes this with the disciples on the road to Emmaus and also with the apostles at the Transfiguration, where despite the presence of Moses (Torah) and Elijah (Prophets), *"they no longer saw anyone except Jesus Himself"* (Mk 9:8). This is what He wants to accomplish with each of us during every Holy Mass!

18. Does Christ truly come in the Liturgy of the Word?
Through the proclamation of the readings of the day, Christ truly comes among us, through the Holy Spirit.
This reality is also reaffirmed by the Second Vatican Council, which states that Christ *"is present in His word, since it is He who speaks when the sacred Scriptures are read in the Church"* (Vat II, SC, 7).

19. What is the purpose of Jesus' coming in the Liturgy of the Word?
Jesus truly comes to every Mass to give us His Grace, to speak personally to us, and to nourish us as He did two thousand years ago when He walked the roads of Galilee and Judea, sowing His Words that are the Holy Spirit and Divine Life. All of this is made visible by the procession with the Gospel Book that takes place before the proclamation of the Gospel.

20. Is there, therefore, a daily Grace given to us?
Yes, every day we have a Word to receive, which is what we ask for in the Our Father when we say: *"Give us today our daily bread"* (Mt 6:11). Even if we have not been able to attend Mass, this Bread has been prepared for us. Jesus comes for all of us, and there is a unique Grace for each one during Mass!

21. What should we do to prevent Grace from passing by us in vain?
We must receive it in our conscience, so as not to lose it and allow it to pass by in vain. Saint Augustine said: *"Timeo Jesum transeuntem"* (I fear the passing Jesus), referring to His Grace; because if I do not listen to it, it passes by, and I lose it. To do *Lectio Divina* every day means not wanting to lose this Grace, sitting down and "eating" the Word received, thus honouring the effort Jesus made to come to us.

3 - Mary is Our Model in Receiving the Word

22. How does Mary receive the Word?
Mary has the perfect ability to receive the Word: she is filled with the Holy Spirit. One could say that Mary's heart—heart in the biblical sense—is the place where the Incarnate Word is born and where it is received and kept.
Mary's docility, her capacity for listening, her receptivity, her silence, her attentiveness, and the Holy Spirit acting in her fully, make her our Model for *Lectio Divina*.
Mary represents the best way to receive the Word. She is truly the Good Soil of the parable of the Sower (cf. Mt 13:3 ff and par.), the only one who received the Word and bore fruit!

23. What is our way of listening to the Word?
If we carefully examine our way of listening to the Word of God, we realise that our hearts are a mix of the first three soils mentioned in the parable of the Sower (cf. Mt 13:3 ff and par.), even though we desire to be like the last soil, "the good soil," to produce fruit. This is a humble and true observation: we do not listen well to the Word; we discover that our hearts are sick, and even the most perfect heart is a mixture of the three unfruitful attitudes.
The words of Christ, abandoned to the hardness of our hearts, are in danger and cannot bear fruit. These words are only half of God's gift; the other half is "the ability to receive them": it is not enough to know that Christ said these things; it is necessary for His words to incarnate in us and produce fruit. Now, the Lord gives us, through His words, also "the ability to receive them," the

"receptivity" typical of Mary; His gift is fundamentally bipolar: He gives the seed and the soil.

Mary's heart is perfect, and God offers it to us freely; it is the first fruit of salvation. Just as to St. John at the foot of the cross, Christ said to every man: *"Behold your mother!"* (Jn 19:27).

24. What should we do with the gift of Mary's heart?

It is up to us to accept this heart, "to use it," to make it our own so that we may be made capable of receiving the Word every day, bearing fruit, and fulfilling life. It is an invitation to imitate St. John and take Mary into our hearts — *"And from that hour the disciple took her to his own home"* (Jn 19:27)— so that, she in us and we in her, we are made capable of receiving the daily Word and putting it into Practice, bearing fruit.

25. What happens when we take Mary into our hearts?

With Mary, the words of Christ find in us their fitting and divine container. "Having Mary available," because God gives her to us, we can, in her and through her, cause the Word of God to bear fruit.

Present at every incarnation of the Word, Mary intercedes for us and, through her prayer, makes us pure in her image, capable of placing the Word of God first in our hearts, and receiving it with Her Fruitfulness.

26. How can we become Mary, the Good Soil?

Through *Lectio*, we progressively become more and more like Mary (in capacity) to receive Jesus in fullness. Mary's docility at the Annunciation and throughout her life becomes ours.

By imitating Mary, day by day, we become like her; our deep being becomes more and more like hers: she lives increasingly in us. The more we invoke her, the more we ask for her help, the more we allow her to guide us and enlighten us, the more we become like her, docile to the action of the Word. Thus, for us too, Mary's heart becomes the place where the Word that is addressed to us every day is born.

In conclusion, our old heart of stone is replaced by the new heart of flesh, a living image of hers, filled with the Holy Spirit: *"I will remove from you your heart of stone and give you a heart of flesh. I will put my spirit within you"* (Ez 36:26-27).

4 - Nourishing Oneself with the Word: Its Necessity, Stages, and Our Responsibility

27. How is the human being made?

Man is a being endowed with a body, a soul, and a spirit, as can be seen in the diagram below. The soul and the spirit (which is its apex) are primarily made up of intelligence and will. In the soul, intelligence and will are active and conscious; they are the visible part of the mountain (below the clouds), whereas in the spirit—comparable to the summit of the mountain, which pierces through the clouds and rises directly towards the sun—intelligence and will are supra-conscious and passive. "Supra-conscious" because consciousness characterises the soul, and "supra" because the spirit is closer to God than the soul: it is capable of participating in divine life as it is, whereas the soul is not. The spirit is passive, because it is moved by God, unlike the soul, which is active and conscious.

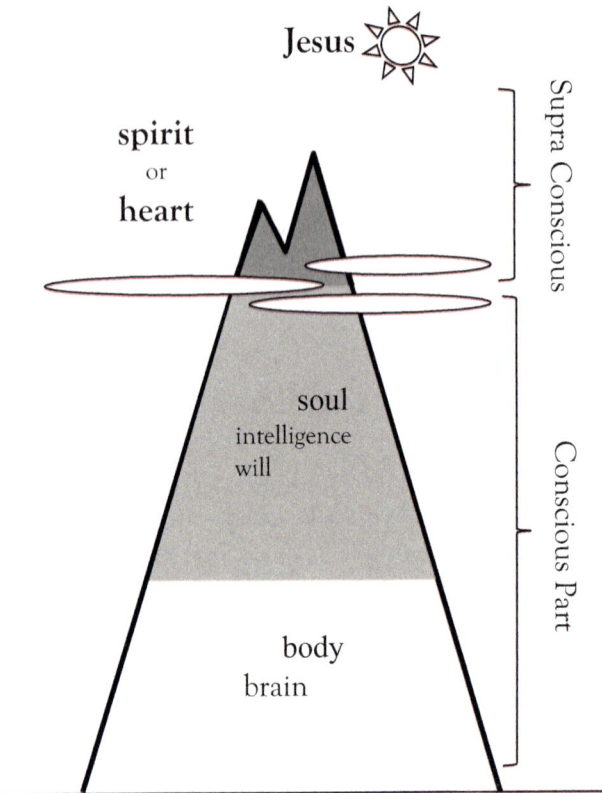

28. What is the true nourishment of intelligence and will?

The true nourishment of the soul, that is, of the active and conscious intelligence and will, is the very Word of God. His Word is a Loving Light: it is Light for our intelligence in its daily activity and Strength and healing for our will. In the desert, when tempted, the Lord responds to the devil, saying: *"Man shall not live by bread alone, but by every word that proceeds from the mouth of God"* (Mt 4:4).

29. Why is it necessary to nourish ourselves with the Word?

We are not made only of body; we also have intelligence and will that need nourishment. Think about it: in our daily lives, we allow our intelligence and will to be nourished by many things and neglect their true daily nourishment, consequently they suffer from terrible atrophy.

We always manage to escape from the Word of God, but when it comes to eating, we never miss the appointment. How reckless! At Mass, at conferences, or retreats, the Word enters one ear and exits the other, but it does not stay within us. If the hen does not delay in incubating the egg, there will be no life; likewise, if we do not preserve the Word in us, if we do not take the time necessary for listening (and, as will be seen, this is a process that needs time, because it is a sacred incarnation), there will be no fruitfulness in our life, neither on earth nor in heaven, because our true life begins on earth when we come into contact with the Word.

Let us then take our portion of Living Bread (the Word of God) every day. It will be our daily bread.

30. What does the process of the descent of the Word into us consist of?

Lectio, or the consumption of the Word, is a process made up of various stages, as shown in the diagram below. The Word of God, in fact, passing through our spirit, progressively descends into the complex soul-body, interacting with it along the way. First, it reaches the intelligence, offering it a clear light little by little, then it crosses the abyss that separates the intelligence from the will, granting the will the strength to incarnate the light it has received.

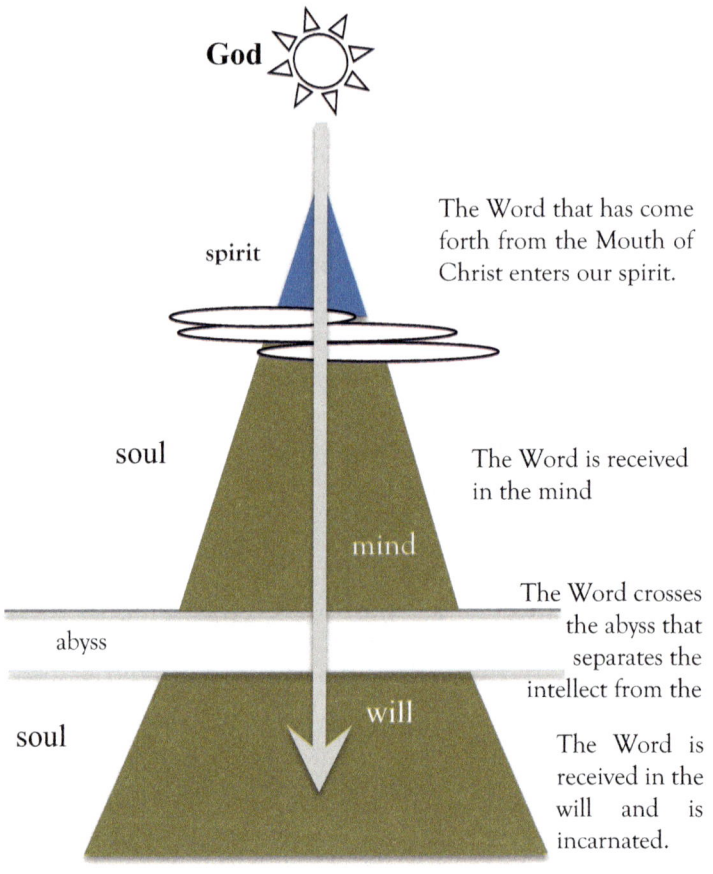

31. Is our collaboration necessary for this descent?

Yes, the Word of God does not act without our collaboration. There is a morsel of Loving Light that we are called to carefully consider each day, to receive in our intelligence, and even more deeply in our conscience, and then allow it to descend into the will, letting it transform us.

It is important for us to facilitate (in the conscience and with the conscience) the path of light and offer it a welcoming ground, accompanying it and giving it a part of ourselves, a space within us, and time. *"Conscience is the most secret core and the sanctuary of a man, where he is alone with God, whose voice echoes in the intimacy"* (Vatican II, *Gaudium et Spes*, 16).

However, God cannot invade our conscience, so it is up to us to make this effort of listening, without which the Word does not enter.

5- The determination to dedicate time; the prayer to find it

32- How much time should be dedicated to *Lectio*?

Since *Lectio* is a true meal and a real incarnation of the Word within us, it takes approximately 55 minutes for all of this to be accomplished within us. Time is needed to eat, chew, digest, and assimilate the Word that Jesus addresses to us today. The process of listening requires time. The entrance of the Loving Light into the various levels of our being (spirit, intelligence, will, body) requires time.

33- Should *Lectio* be done every day?

Yes, although it can be quite a challenge to fit an hour of *Lectio* into each day, given the many commitments.

However, the first step is to firmly believe in the right we have to receive a Word from God every day, just as we receive bread every day.

34- And those who cannot?

If we are convinced of the paramount importance of *Lectio* but think we cannot find time for it in our day, and this causes discomfort or sadness, we might say a simple prayer to the Lord:

"Lord, you have made me understand that it is important to meet with you and listen to you every day in the readings of the Mass, but you see that the time I have available does not allow me to do this. Since you

desire to speak to me and you are Omnipotent, I offer you my time, my life, my plans; may you organise my life and my day. Help me understand how I can find time, how to use the time you give me. Show me by what means I can reorder my life, remove what burdens it, and preserve what is good; help me find sacred time to meet with you."

Let us raise this prayer with all our hearts, repeat it from time to time, trust in the Lord, and then open our eyes: He will show us many things, and the results will soon follow.

35- Is it therefore essential to entrust ourselves to the Lord?
Yes, if we want Christ to be the Master and Guide of our lives, our Spouse – this is the meaning of Baptism – it is necessary to entrust ourselves completely to Him, to lay ourselves bare and open our conscience to His voice, without conditions.

Christ wants to take our lives into His hands; He is our True Physician and knows us better than we know ourselves. To place our entire life in His hands, to let Him lead and transform it, this is what He desires us to do! This is the implicit starting point of *Lectio*. If we have not yet truly given our lives to the Lord, if we have not yet committed ourselves seriously to Him, we are still owners of ourselves and our time. In that case, *Lectio* would end up being "time given to the Lord," not a lifelong commitment, not a commitment of the entire day. The difference is enormous!

36- Do we need to make a decision then?
Yes, placing our hand in that of Christ is a fundamental point, a turning point in our life, a great decision to be made, so beautiful and so radical.

Therefore, it is important to stop, reflect, and take some time in silence before Christ in the Tabernacle to consider the matter, its absolute importance for us, for our lives.

This decision should not frighten us, because it will truly make us free. Christ rightly says that His yoke is easy and His burden is light (cf. Mt 11:30)! We give Him everything, this is Wisdom! Nothing will remain for us but to let ourselves be guided by Christ, do the tasks of the day, and sleep in Peace! It is this strong and radical medicine that will make us truly happy! Let us love the Truth above all things, it will grant us True Joy!

Let us then place our "yes" in Mary's "yes." This is the Only Way to have a "yes" worthy of Christ and one that will please Him.

Part II- The Practice of *Lectio Divina*

37- How can we summarise *Lectio Divina*?

Lectio Divina can be summarised in the following 7 steps:

1. **Sit** in a quiet and solitary place; if possible, in the morning; place yourself in the Presence of the Lord Jesus.
2. **Ask the Holy Spirit** to enable you to listen to the Lord: "What do you want from me, Lord, today?" / "Give me Your Light."
3. **Repeat** the reading of the two or three texts - renewing your desire (through prayer) to discover the will of Jesus - until they offer a single, clear, and practical light for me today.
4. **Ask** for the strength of the Holy Spirit to enable you to put into practice the light received: "Give me Your Strength to put into practice the Word received."
5. Briefly **write down** the "light" received.
6. **Put into practice the Word received today**.
7. At the end of the day, **check** and joyfully thank the Lord Jesus for having fulfilled, with the strength of His Spirit, His Word received during *Lectio Divina*.

38- Is it possible to further summarise these 7 steps?

Yes, all of *Lectio Divina* can indeed be summarised in two questions and one action:
- The first question is: "Lord, give me Your Holy Spirit to understand what You want from me today."
- The second question (once we understand what is being asked of us) is: "Lord, give me Your Holy Spirit to incarnate and accomplish what You have asked of me."

The essence of the Theology of Listening is contained in these two questions (which can be summarised by the words of Mary: "Behold the servant of the Lord; let it be done to me according to Your Word." [Lk 1:38]) and the subsequent putting into practice, with the Lord's strength, of the Word received.

1- How to practise *Lectio Divina*

39- How should we physically position ourselves to begin the *Lectio*?

One should begin the *Lectio* by sitting in a quiet and solitary place, preferably in the morning, holding the two (or three) readings from the Mass of the day (these can be found in a personal Bible with the help of a liturgical calendar, or in the Missal, or even online, on specific websites). We may place an Icon of the Lord and/or a lit candle in front of us. This serves as a reminder that we are attempting to listen to the Lord, who desires to speak to us.

40- What is the first step to take when holding the Word of God?

We must become aware that we are before the Lord Jesus, the Risen One, present in our room. We should then place ourselves in His presence, face to face with Him, considering the love He has for us and His desire to speak to us today, to change us, and to give us His life through His Word, which is Spirit and Life.

41- What is the role of the Holy Spirit in *Lectio Divina*?

The Holy Spirit's role is vital. It is essential to ask for the help of the Holy Spirit in order to listen to the Lord's Word and put it into practice. Throughout the process of listening, we should constantly and insistently ask for the Holy Spirit, as He is the driving force. Without the Holy Spirit, we cannot "see" the Lord nor listen to Him.

42- Which reading should we start with?

We can start with the first reading, simply following the order in which the readings are proclaimed during Mass. However, this is not an absolute condition.

43- What should we do when we have the First Reading in our hands?

After asking the Holy Spirit to help us listen to Jesus, we read slowly, with attention and listening, 4 or 5 times through the first reading, occasionally repeating our first question: "Tell me what you want from me, Lord."

As we read and discover the text, we should aim to understand its meaning with a minimum of clarity, also helping ourselves with footnotes, though we should not linger excessively on them.

The main purpose of this repeated reading is to listen to the Lord, who will use a word or a verse to begin speaking to us.

On Sundays, feast days, solemnities, and other occasions, there are three readings. In this case, we repeat with the second reading what we did with the first. Some people also add the Psalm—this is not a problem, as the action of the Holy Spirit remains the same.

44- After taking the Gospel of the day, what should we do?

We read the Gospel of the Day slowly, 4 or 5 times, always focusing on the Lord and saying: "Tell me what you want from me." Again, we should aim to understand the text first, its meaning, and possibly delve into a new word.

45- How long does the initial reading of the two texts last?

This attentive and slow reading can take about 20 to 40 minutes (though we do not look at the clock; we are before the Risen Lord!).

46- What is experienced in this first phase of repeated reading?

Often, if the first reading is taken from a difficult text (as many from the Old Testament are), we may not feel anything special during this first phase of the *Lectio*: the supernatural light does not yet appear. Therefore, we should not be surprised if we do not gain anything yet or if we remain hesitant in discerning the Word-food we are to receive.

In fact, at most, when the text is more understandable (as many from the New Testament often are), we emerge from this repeated reading with more than one possibility, that is, with various "lights"/ideas in the text.

Practically speaking, it often happens that the Lord does not give anything in this phase, and there is almost a daily appearance of a "wall" at this point in the *Lectio*. That is, we read the two texts (the first reading and the Gospel), and nothing emerges: we notice various ideas in the two texts, but we are not looking for ideas, not even ideas that converge. We are preparing to receive a Word that comes from the mouth of the Lord to enter us, passing through the two texts.

47- What should we do when faced with this "wall" of God's apparent silence?

Often the Lord wants to bring us to this wall, a wall of the impossible (cf. Mt 19:26), because He truly wants to see, through our persistence, our choice, our determination to desire His will and put Him first.

Lectio Divina is not just an activity of the mind, but of the conscience: it is a daily gift from the Lord, which must be asked for, using our minds and our whole being, and of which we experience the gratuity every day.

Therefore, when we reach this wall of "aridity," facing the two texts, we should not despair. Instead, in a strong leap of faith, *"hoping against all hope"* (Rom 4:18), we accept to go one more mile (cf. Mt 5:41) with the Lord, asking Him once again: "Tell me what you want from me today." We thus open our conscience more fully to the action of the Spirit, who helps us pass through the wall of the impossible, allowing us to experience the flow of His Grace. It is a daily experience!

48- When does the supernatural light begin to manifest itself?

The Gospel is the book par excellence that speaks to us directly about Jesus. Often, it is during the reading of the Gospel of the day that the supernatural light of God begins to manifest to our conscience through a word or a verse. Remember that during Mass, we stand to listen to the Gospel, because the Lord is truly present among us and speaks to each one of us. This shows the power that characterises the reading of the Gospel.

Sometimes more than one passage speaks to us, and we hesitate between the different lights. The power of the Gospel is such that often the text speaks in more than one place. It may also happen that the reading reminds us of other lights we have received from this text in the past.

49- How does the supernatural light manifest itself?

We do not see anything physical in the text. We only have a very clear and somewhat strong impression (as we repeat the reading, asking for the light of the Holy Spirit) that the text is no longer uniform, but that one word (or more) or one verse (or more) speaks more directly to our conscience than the rest. It is as though the Lord is highlighting these words with a highlighter, and they speak to us more.

50- Among two or more lights, how can we discern which is the true Light for today?

We may emerge from the Gospel reading with various possibilities:

a) We have only one light, but we are not yet sure that it is the one from God (it may be the light from a previous *Lectio Divina*, and not the light for today).

b) We have two lights, one of which is the true light, and the other is not—being only a concept that speaks to us or that we like.

c) We have more than two lights, and only one is the one that comes from above.

To sift through the harvest of this first gathering, we need to return to the first reading (which often, remember, does not give much as supernatural light) and reread it. But this time, we do so with these lights or doubts (a, b, c) within us. We then begin to read, making a back-and-forth movement, comparing the two texts.

This movement is done while we are before the Lord, who seeks, using both texts, to speak to us and give us a single light. One Lord, one heart reading (us), and thus one light. The presence of two or more texts changes nothing about the uniqueness of the light/bite to be received from Him.

51- How do we make the first movement of return to the first reading?

We begin by grasping the light(s) received from the Gospel and going with them to read the first reading, waiting (as we read), without forcing (without projecting our thoughts or desires or literal similarities between the texts), for the first reading to begin to "move," to "animate," to give us a light as well.

This light that emerges, which passes through a word or a verse we have already read several times, is a supernatural "stained-glass window" effect, very captivating. Through it, the Lord shows us how each word of the text is like a diamond, capable of reflecting His light in various ways, while still being the same word and respecting the historical context of the reading.

52- What happens as we continue this "back-and-forth" movement?

To ensure it is the Lord speaking to us (and not our own thoughts), we continue to make a back-and-forth movement between the texts, and especially between the words that begin to strike us here and there.

We will notice that the Light the Lord gives us begins to emerge as unified. It is from one text to another, focusing more and more only on the words the Lord uses today, that we feel the Light pass through.

The one light passes, and Christ's message for us (in its broad lines) becomes clear.

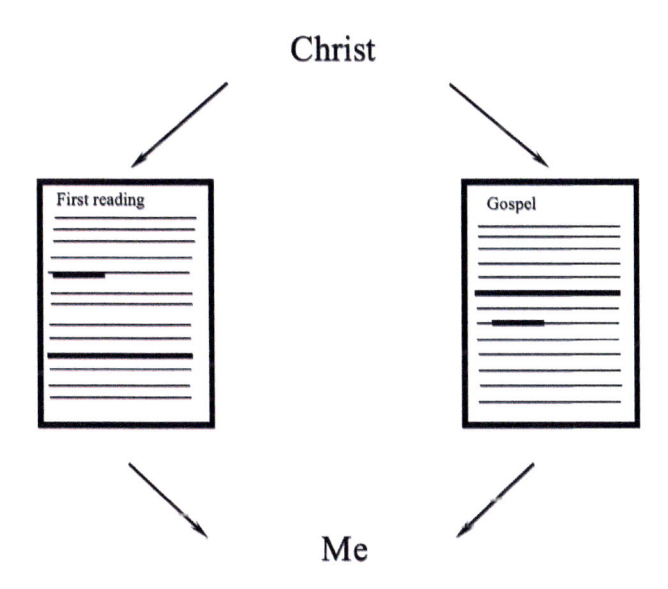

53- Is it enough to see a single light to know what to do?

No, it is necessary to allow this light to become clearer and more practical. This is the purpose of *Lectio Divina*: to understand well what the Lord wants from us and not abandon Him, or abandon *Lectio Divina*, until His will for us today becomes precise.

The Lord Jesus may ask us:
- An act purely interior (such as entrusting to Him a burden, a concern, or welcoming a person into our hearts);
- An act both interior and exterior at the same time (such as forgiving someone who has wronged us and reconciling with them);
- An act only exterior (such as doing something that an acquaintance or spouse has been asking us to do for some time or that would please them).
This act, however small, is impossible through our own strength alone.

54- How should we proceed to put this precise light into practice?
This is where the second question comes: "Lord, You have shown me what You are asking me to do, now give me Your strength, Your Holy Spirit, to be able to put it into practice."
At this point, with the grace of the Lord, it is possible to put the received Word into practice. The practice can happen immediately if it is an interior act, whereas if it is an exterior act, it must obviously happen outside the context of the hour of *Lectio Divina*.
At the end, we thank the Lord for His daily Gift of taking care of us and giving us a Word of Life and Healing.
Before getting up, it is important to briefly write down the light received. Writing down, crystallising on paper what has been received in the depths of the heart, helps. Even if we limit ourselves to writing only the words we received, we help the light to incarnate in our lives. We hold onto the word to prevent it

from dispersing; we gather it so that it may retain all its practical efficacy in our lives.

55- Is there a relationship between the day and the light received?
Often, the Holy Spirit points out various connections between the light received and the events of the day. The day is often spent under the strong light of the *Lectio*, a light that directs it, encompasses it, and elevates it.

56- What should we do at the end of the day?
At the end of the day, it is important to review its flow with God's help, doing something like an examination of conscience with the essential criterion of the initial light, measuring the day against this light. We thank the Lord if we have been able to put into practice the Word received.

2- Let us delve deeper into *Lectio Divina*

57- What is the benefit of a more in-depth analysis of the *Lectio Divina* process?
Understanding better what happens within us during *Lectio Divina* is very helpful in the long run. For various reasons, the initial simplicity of listening to the Lord through His Word often becomes weakened over time or even drained of its supernatural essence. To avoid this pitfall, it is important to review our approach to *Lectio* (much like we review our day by making an examination of conscience). The aim is to improve the practice, correct any mistakes, and become more aware both of the Gift that God gives us through *Lectio Divina* and of the demands it entails.

A deeper understanding of the inner mechanisms of *Lectio* and an exploration of the theology of listening are fundamental acts for the Christian, acts in which one must become an expert.

58- What is the first aspect that needs to be checked in our practice of *Lectio Divina*?

When we engage in *Lectio*, the first thing we must check is that we perform the following act of faith: *"The Holy Spirit is the Author of the Scriptures." "Everything that the inspired authors or sacred writers assert is to be considered as asserted by the Holy Spirit"* (Vatican II, *Dei Verbum*, 11). If we remember this, we are greatly helped to express our act of faith, opening our inner ear to listen to God who has written those words.

The Holy Spirit is also the Interpreter of the Scriptures. Only the author of a letter can explain its meaning, and the Holy Spirit is the author of that letter, which is Sacred Scripture. Therefore, we must persistently turn to Him to understand its meaning or meanings: *"Ask, and it will be given to you; seek, and you will find; knock, and it will be opened to you"* (Mt 7:7). A reading of Sacred Scripture "according to the Spirit" is therefore necessary.

59- What are the criteria for reading "according to the Spirit"?

The Church – through the "Fathers of the Church" – offers us three criteria for reading the Scriptures "in the Holy Spirit," which it is good to refer to during *Lectio*, as if they were a new instinct we feel within ourselves. Here are the criteria:

1. *"Give great attention to 'the content and unity of all of Scripture';*
2. *Read Scripture within the 'living Tradition of the whole Church';*
3. *Be attentive to the 'analogy of faith,' meaning the coherence of the truths of faith with one another and within the entirety of the plan of Revelation."* (CCC 112)

The Holy Spirit is our Guide and Teacher: we truly need the Holy Spirit, the understanding He gives us to comprehend the Scriptures. By invoking the Spirit, we open our understanding to the gift that comes from above. It is something absolutely indispensable and important that may seem completely new to someone who has never experienced it, because they are used to working only with the light of their own intelligence, which is necessary but insufficient.

60- What other aspect should we verify in our practice of *Lectio Divina*?

We need to verify our inner attitude. At the beginning of *Lectio*, it is essential to mentally free ourselves from distractions, offering them to the Lord, and giving all priority to Christ, who wishes to speak to us, without putting anything before Him.

Then, as a response to the Gift that Jesus is about to give us, we must prepare ourselves by offering Him all of our being, unconditionally, gathering all our energy to Listen to Him as He speaks to us through the readings of the day.

To do this, it is indispensable to ask for the help of Mary. We can then recite a short prayer like the following: *Give us, Mary, your purity in listening, your attachment to the Word of your Son, your commitment to putting it into practice with the strength of the Holy Spirit.*

61- What does the first phase of repeated reading of the two texts accomplish in us?

This effort, made with the general help of grace, allows us to understand what needs to be understood today in the text, to "exhaust" its meanings, to grasp them, to do our best and thus reach the surface of the water, the point of encounter with the direct and personal action of the Spirit of Christ. Every day, in fact, there is the need to understand just enough to move forward.

Not so little that *Lectio* becomes sterile, nor so much that it prevents its dynamism.

The words understood are like the keys of a piano freed from the cloth that covered them or like the sails of a ship unfurled. The Spirit can then blow, play, speak, make His Voice heard.

62- How do we "encourage" the Word to reveal itself?

However, the Word, to begin to reveal itself, needs to see a complete desire from us, it wants to see the humility of Mary in us, our persistent asking. Only this "provokes" God, "pushes" Him, "wins" Him (wins His Heart) and makes Him descend.

Often, the first phase of reading the texts (especially if one of these is from the Old Testament) does not yield results, as has been seen. We have the impression of hitting a wall, the wall of God's silence. At this point, it is necessary to want to go an extra mile with the Lord (cf. Mt 5:41). It is necessary to gather all our strength and ask the Lord once more to help us understand what He desires from us today, saying: "What do you want from me, Lord, today?", "Give me Your Light so I can take a step with You." This is the first question, the most important, because everything in *Lectio* depends on it.

Then begins a more intense phase of listening, during which the action of the Spirit, from being general, becomes direct and personal, and our attitude also changes.

From this moment on, in fact, we need to take a certain distance from the texts, while still continuing to read them, to see through them in transparency (as with a stained-glass window) and allow Christ to take possession of them and use them to speak to us.

We should not work on the text with our intellect (this would lead to projection or intellectualism). We must do our best to become receptive: this is the most difficult thing.

It is not just about silencing the intellect, but about making it docile to the text – like a photographic film sensitive to light –

waiting for a word, a phrase, to speak to us, to come alive, to become brighter, more intense than the others. The help of the Holy Spirit and the direct intervention of Mary make this supernatural operation of Listening effective.

63- How do we obtain a single Light?
Every day, the Lord gives us a Bite, a Divine Meal. It is a Light that He gives us, and this is to change us, to help us take one step at a time (*"Each day has enough trouble of its own"* [Mt 6:34]).

The light requires time to pass from the spirit to the soul, and at first, it does not appear. Later, often more understandings of the text appear, but we do not yet know how to distinguish between the "understanding of the text" (the normal result of an effort to read, of exegetical deepening) and the "Light" that is supernaturally given by God, which begins to show itself.

The understanding of the text is the result of our effort and comes somehow from below. On the other hand, the Light that He gives us comes from above and, at first, as it begins to rise, it seems weak and almost confuses itself with the lights of exegetical understanding of the text.

The discernment of the Light happens thanks to the presence of the two or three texts, because they must cross paths at a point. After several readings, the Light begins to pass through one text (it often starts with the Gospel, because it is more powerful, it has a special Grace from the Presence of Christ) and vaguely through the other.

After reading the other text a few times, continuing to ask for God's will, the Light already perceived in the first text begins to confirm, intensify, and clarify. We then obtain a single Light. The two texts, through certain passages that we can transcribe into a small notebook, no longer reveal more than one supernatural Light, which is given to us.

It is Christ who truly begins to speak to us, as indicated in the diagram below.

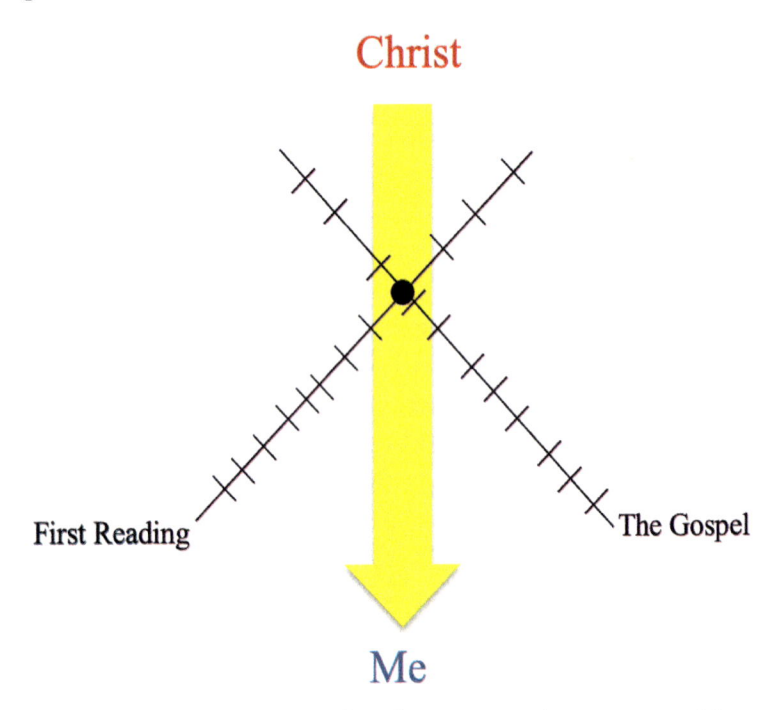

Christ

First Reading　　　　　The Gospel

Me

The text provides a profound reflection on the process of *Lectio Divina* and the way divine illumination works within the soul. Here's a summary of the key ideas from your passage:

63- How to obtain a single Light?
Each day, God gives us a divine "bite" of food, a light intended to transform us. Initially, it's difficult to distinguish between intellectual comprehension of the text and the supernatural light God offers. Over time, as we continue our reading and ask for God's will, this light begins to grow clearer, confirming and intensifying, showing us one unified, divine light. This process of illumination enables us to hear Christ speaking directly to us through the Scriptures.

64- How to make the Light distinct?

The process continues with repeated reading of the words that touch us, asking: "What do You want from me, Lord, today, practically and concretely?" As we reflect more deeply, the light becomes clearer and more distinct, guiding us to a specific action or point where God's wisdom desires to transform us. This light becomes personal and distinct, and writing it down can help to clarify and shape it further.

65- How to discern the Light received?

To discern whether the light is from God, the texts will converge on a single word, a miraculous moment of God's grace. This word becomes a beacon, confirming that the illumination is genuine.

66- What are the characteristics of the Light received?

The light has four main characteristics:

1. **Newness**: It's a fresh illumination, not originating from ourselves, but from God.
2. **Concreteness**: The light calls us to action, whether interior (e.g., a new understanding of God) or exterior (e.g., reconciling with someone).
3. **Smallness**: The act required might seem small in the grand scheme, but it holds immense importance.
4. **Impossibility**: Despite its simplicity, the action the light requires is beyond our own strength to carry out; it reveals the gap between our intellect and will.

67- Can the descent of the Light in us be represented?

Yes, the diagram illustrates this process. The initial question, represented by an arrow ascending toward God, symbolises our desire for guidance. The descending arrow represents God's response, pointing to a specific area of our will He wants to heal and transform. The grace begins to work in our intellect, helping us to recognise the action we are called to take, which, though small, is impossible without God's intervention.

This process is an ongoing dynamic of opening oneself to God's word, surrendering to His will, and allowing the light to guide us in small but transformative steps. The act of surrender and openness to God's will are essential for the effectiveness of *Lectio Divina*.

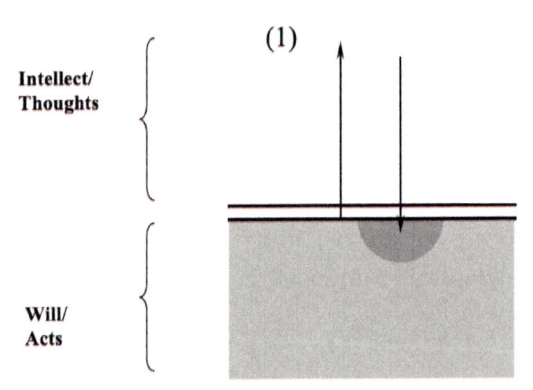

(1)

Intellect/ Thoughts

Will/ Acts

68- How to act in the face of our inability to accomplish the task?

After asking the Lord what He wants from us, He points to our will, asking for a specific action. The surprising realisation is that this action seems impossible to perform with our own strength (as in Matthew 19:25). In response to this impossibility, we must make a second request to the Lord: to grant us the Holy Spirit to help us put His Word into practice, praying:

"Lord, give me Your strength to fulfil the Word I have received."
Once we make this second request, the Lord provides His strength, giving us the necessary impulse to carry out what He has asked. It is through His grace that we are enabled to act.

When this light penetrates our will, healing and transforming it, we experience God's Word in a new way—it becomes a deep knowledge of God. At this moment, God is born in us, not merely in the intellect, but in both the intellect and the will, as they work in union. This signifies the transition from intellectual knowledge to contemplative knowledge of God, as we begin to savour and experience the truth incarnated within us.

The diagram below illustrates how the arrow from the second question descends through the abyss between the intellect and the will, healing the will in a small but significant way.

This process reflects the transformation of the soul as both the intellect and the will are united in God's grace, enabling us to perform what we thought was impossible. The journey from knowledge to contemplation is complete when both faculties are fully engaged, leading to a deeper encounter with God.

This illustrates the core of *Lectio Divina* as an experiential journey—God's Word becomes not just something we understand, but something we live, experience, and taste through the action of His grace.

Intellect/ Thoughts

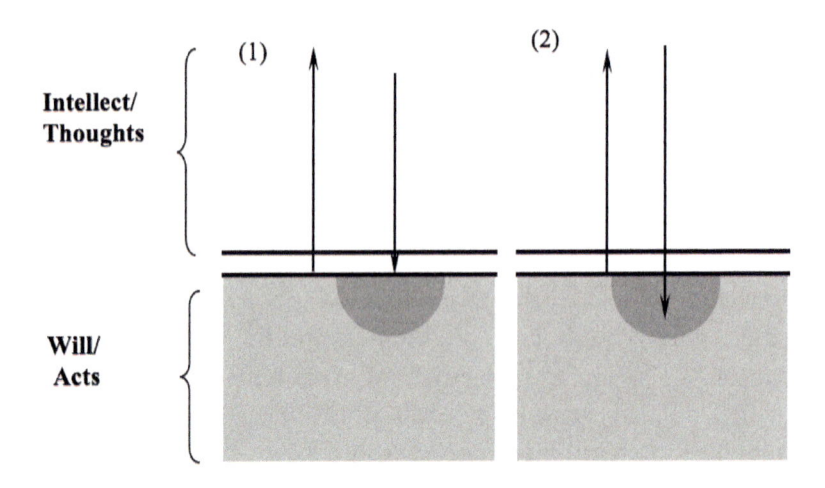

(1) (2)

Will/ Acts

69- Can we then accomplish the act?

Yes, once the will has been healed in a particular area, it can now perform a new, synergistic act. This act is the fruit of our encounter with Jesus and is a small step taken with His strength. This act is essential, as it completes the journey of the Word received. The Word begins from the highest heavens, from the very heart of the Trinity, and reaches the deepest part of our being, our body, through the concrete action we take. Thus, the Word unites heaven and earth within us.

70- Can *Lectio Divina* be sterile?

Yes, it is important to ensure that the Word we receive, like a small sphere of light coming from God's mouth, truly incarnates. Otherwise, *Lectio Divina* will not bear fruit.

Sometimes, without realising it, we may approach the text in a sterile manner, receiving it only in a way that feeds the intellect without transforming the will. This leads to the Word not completing its course.

A "well-done" *Lectio Divina*, however, allows the Word to incarnate, becoming an experience, knowledge, healing, and transformation of the will.

Our enemies (the world, the flesh, and Satan) attempt to stop the Word from reaching our lower parts (our will, senses, and body), preventing it from changing, healing, or saving us. Without this transformation, Baptism remains incomplete.

When we practise *Lectio Divina*, in a certain sense, our enemies are always present, doing their work to prevent today's Portion from taking flesh in us! They constantly and tirelessly seek to render sterile the Work of God, which is always an Incarnation.

71- Must the Word sown in us bear fruit?

Yes, and in the Parable of the Sower (Matthew 13, Mark 4, Luke 8), we see that only in Mary, the "Good Soil," does the seed (the Word, the Bite) bear fruit. Satan has no place in Mary. All attempts in the other three types of soil fail to yield fruit, leaving them sterile.

Thus, when we pray in the *Our Father* "lead us not into temptation," we are essentially saying, "Lord, place me in Mary, and prevent me from falling into the temptation of stepping outside of her, the Good Soil." If we were to step outside, our *Lectio Divina* would be sterile, and the Word would remain "un-incarnated" in us.

"Lead us not into temptation," that is, make us strong, grant us Your Grace so that, with Mary and like Mary, we may allow the Word, today's Portion (the Bread of today), to be incarnated in us! Grant us Your Grace so that we may not listen to Satan, who seeks each day to render Your Portion sterile, "un-incarnated"! Grant us Your Grace so that we may make way, make room, and safeguard Your Word as it descends into us, until it is put into practice.

72- What happens when we have accomplished the act?

Through the act we perform, a part of Jesus incarnates in us. The Holy Spirit, together with Mary, carries out this work within us: the birth of the new man, day by day. This is a slow but effective action.

Each day, we walk with grace in true friendship, learning to cooperate with God, adapting our being to His action, and working synergistically with Him.

At the end of the day, we need to verify whether we have incarnated the Word received and thank the Lord for enabling us, through His Spirit, to accomplish the Word during *Lectio Divina*.

This should be our only joy, even if we are full of imperfections and sins. Firmly and daily accomplishing what He asks means allowing the Lord to hold the thread of our lives, so that, with time, He may possess us completely.

73- How can we summarise *Lectio Divina* at the end of this analysis?

The analysis of *Lectio Divina* enriches its practice, bringing to light new points that were previously implicit. The entire process can be summarised as follows:

The text outlines how the encounter with the Word moves beyond mere intellectual understanding into transformative experience, where both the intellect and the will cooperate with God's grace to make the Word incarnate in the believer's life. This deepened understanding emphasises that *Lectio Divina* is not just about reading or meditating on Scripture but about allowing it to shape and heal the will, leading to genuine spiritual growth.

I- Preparation

1. **Sit down** – Create a physical space of stillness and openness.
2. **Place yourself in the presence of Christ** – Consciously become aware of Christ's nearness.
3. **Reflect on Christ's desire to speak to you** – Know that He wants to communicate personally with you.
4. **Give absolute priority to Christ** – Set aside all distractions to focus on Him.
5. **Surrender to Him unconditionally** – Offer yourself entirely to His will.

II- Listening

6. **Read to understand** – Absorb the text at a surface level with the intent to understand.
7. **Read to uncover Christ's will** – Seek His message in the words.
8. **Read to gain a single guiding light** – Look for a revelation or insight from the passage.
9. **Read again to make the light clearer** – Allow the truth to become distinct and take shape.
10. **Write down the words that resonate with you** – Note the phrases or ideas that speak to your heart.

III- Putting into Practice

11. **Ask the Holy Spirit to help you put the Word into action** – Recognise the need for divine assistance.
12. **Give thanks, immersed in Him** – Offer your thanks to God, fully immersed in His presence and grace.
13. **Put into practice the Word you've received today** – Take concrete steps to live out the Word.
14. **Pay attention to the resonances of the Word throughout the day** – Notice how the Word continues to speak to you.
15. **Offer thanks at the end of the day** – Give thanks for the grace of the Word and for the guidance it has provided.

Part III – The Effort of *Lectio Divina* and the Fruits That Come From it

1- Entering through the Narrow Door

74 – What effort does *Lectio* require?
What *Lectio* requires is an effort of humility, of descent. This effort must be made, and only then will the Lord make Himself known. Everything superficial must be eliminated in order to descend into the depth of consciousness, to humble oneself inwardly and, in this way, to be able to listen to the Lord and not to ourselves. This is the purity of heart. The Lord reveals Himself only to the pure: *"Blessed are the pure in heart, for they shall see God"* (Mt 5:8). The purity required is not substantial but attitudinal; otherwise, if total purity were necessary to meet the Lord, no one would encounter Him. Since it is an attitudinal purity, we ourselves can control it and decide to have it; we possess the means to this purity, it depends on us. Certainly, without the grace of God, we cannot do anything, but the Lord always guarantees us the grace to realise this purity of listening. It is clear: we must ask for the Holy Spirit, who, with His strength, allows us to hear the voice of the Lord.

75 – Why is our listening often superficial?
Indeed, our listening is often superficial and the effort we are called to make in listening reveals to the Lord our freely renewed choice every day. On the one hand, we are willing to listen only to what pleases us; on the other hand, our capacity for listening is determined by how much we are willing to give to the Lord. Frequently, we do not want to give everything. We give time, money, part of ourselves, but certain areas of our soul are closed to the Lord. We forget that the Lord does not ask for time or money; or rather, He wants much more than a little time or money: He wants us. Through *Lectio*, He wants to "eat us"–little by little, but totally.

Our freedom is the most precious thing in His eyes; He waits for us to offer it to Him freely; He desires that this gift be made often and renewed: it is His most ardent desire. By offering ourselves to Him every day, we come to hear His voice and let His Word act in us and through us. In this way, the Word of God penetrates deep into our being, and *Lectio* can take place. The quality of listening, its "purity," is determined by a fundamental disposition that must be renewed: the unconditional gift of oneself, which produces the impetus that allows the Word of God to enter into us. Let us ask the Lord to help us offer ourselves to Him so that we can listen to and follow Him every day.

76 – What other attitude is necessary for the purity of listening?
Another point to underline is the importance of insistence in asking the Lord to reveal to us what He wants from us today. The first question will always remain the key to *Lectio*, its difficulty, its battleground. It would be more accurate to say not "the first question," but "the quality of the first question." We must know how to insist with God. Insistence and stubbornness do not bore the good Lord, but they work something crucial in our hearts: they purify them. This insistence urges us to gather all our energies, the scattered energies of our hearts, to direct them towards God. Insisting while begging frees our hearts from all obstacles. Let us observe the following diagram. (See the diagram on the opposite page.)

The heart is represented by the vessel; the stones present in the heart are the attachments to many things.

These things seem to have materialised in the heart, occupying a place that does not belong to them. In reality, problems exist outside of us, but our attachment to them makes them live within us. Our heart is filled with countless objects, while it should be occupied only by its Creator.

Collect all the heart's energies

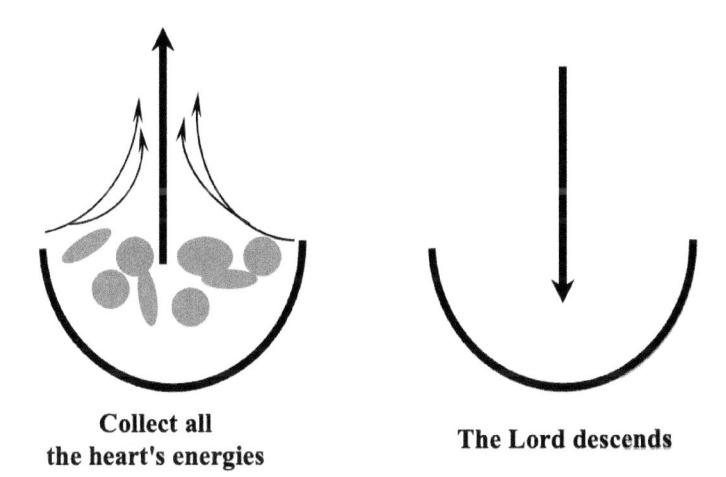

The Lord descends

In the Virgin Mary, only God dwelled, because she desired only Him: this is the reason for her purity and her poverty of spirit. At this level, purity, humility, and poverty are equivalent. We are invited to imitate Mary and her purity, which captivated God. He was pleased with her total and unconditional availability to His will. In this way, Mary drew God into her womb; this is the power she has over God Himself. Mary gives us her heart, her purity, so that we can imitate her. Through this question, asked with all our heart in *Lectio*, we purify our hearts, and it is needless to add that the Lord, as soon as He sees purity in us, a free heart, rushes to us. As soon as He sees Mary, the humble, in a heart, He comes, answers, and does not delay. Blessed is the pure heart that, like and with Mary's, will hear the word of the Lord every day and put it into practice!

Lectio, therefore, is a battle; the fiercest: the battle between the new man and the old man within us.

77 – Is it possible to do *Lectio* without a genuine desire for conversion?

No, because the desire for conversion is the heart of *Lectio*. Every person has the duty to seek the truth and then to conform their life to it. Sin consists not only in failing to conform life to the truth known, but even before that, in not seeking the truth (within our being, there exists not only the abyss between the intellect and the will but also the one between the intellect and God).

In the knowledge of truth, there is an incessant journey, which constitutes the commitment of a lifetime, because it means progressively entering into Christ, who is the truth; it is a constant revelation, an illumination. This is the foundation of *Lectio*: a progressive revelation, which presupposes the desire for change. Indeed, one can physically do *Lectio*, but if one does not desire conversion, it is useless. For Scripture to nourish the soul and spirit, it is essential to be determined to let oneself be shaken, converted, turned upside down, to accept being illuminated by what we read, without seeking our own interest. He who is convinced he sees does not need the doctor; Christ can give him nothing and continues on His way. But he who believes that Christ is the light; he who knows that he can take a step forward, for this act of faith, will progress. Through an act of faith (in Christ as the doctor and saviour), one moves from knowing (Christ has more light than I do) to a knowledge ("experience" of the illumination brought by Christ).

Lectio is, therefore, an act of faith, an invitation to move, every day, from a subjective truth to an objective truth, from a level of perception and progress in the truth towards a greater truth. It is a moving away from one's subjectivity towards objective light. This is the price that must be paid to effect daily conversion and allow Christ to grow in us through the work of the Holy Spirit (who takes us out of ourselves and enables us to receive the light) and with the consent of Mary.

78 – Is *Lectio* an exercise of love?

Yes, *Lectio* is a true exercise of love because it requires that, every day, we step outside ourselves to lovingly, courageously, and authentically seek the truth. *Lectio* is for souls that love the truth and are not afraid of to face it; it seeks generous and courageous souls, capable of questioning themselves daily before God in order to be converted. To love God is simply to do His will. The search for this will is the heart of *Lectio*, as we have seen. *"If you love Me, you will keep My commandments"* (John 14:15), *"whoever has My commandments and keeps them is the one who loves Me."* (John 14:21, see also v. 23)

79 – Does doing *Lectio* mean digging deep?

Yes, doing *Lectio* means digging deep and laying foundations. The more one practises *Lectio*, the deeper one digs, the more one penetrates into the depths of our being, the more one allows God to descend into us. In fact, it is we who either allow or prevent God from entering deeply into us: it depends on the quality of our listening. It is necessary to dig deep, to descend into ourselves, to let the light penetrate into our shadowy areas, into our deepest roots, into our darkness. It is up to us whether we open the door to Him or not: it is our freedom, our willingness to descend, that decides. All of this comes at a cost, but it depends solely on us. Our task is to confront the light, to allow ourselves to be illuminated by the light that is the word of God today. To look at the Word face to face, to confront it, to swallow it, to assimilate it: this requires a great love for the truth and a courageous attitude, a spiritual courage, a desire for the light to overcome our darkness.

2- The Temptations to Escape

80 – What is the first temptation among the most common ones?
There are various temptations to escape that present themselves and press upon us at this moment. They must be rejected with determination. *Lectio* is the ascetic exercise par excellence; its effort is to remain under the light of Scripture, of Christ who speaks to us. **The first temptation**, superficial in nature, is the desire to **do something different** that could be done at another time. The idea of writing a letter or engaging in something else will try to dissuade us from exposing ourselves to the light of Christ, because the devil, just like us, at the deepest core of our being, wishes to avoid this light. So, here is the effort we must make: to endure and strive to place ourselves on the narrow road that leads to liberation and true transformation.

81 – Another widespread temptation?
The second temptation – a deeper one – is to reveal or expose **only part of** ourselves to Christ. This attitude clearly reflects a lack of purity. When we go to the doctor, we are not ashamed to show him our wound or wounds. Similarly, we must let Christ act freely, presenting ourselves to Him as we are, asking Him to do as He wishes.

82 – What if we think we already know the text?
One might also think that they already know the text and become bored, even before starting to read it. This too is a temptation! An act of faith must be made: faith that this is the word of God, that God will speak to me today in a new way. The same text speaks differently depending on the person who listens to it and the stage or spiritual moment in which the person finds themselves. The word of God walks with the believer and offers them what they

need in a specific spiritual situation. It is essential to believe this to overcome the temptation.

83 – Are notes and commentaries a "potential danger"?
Yes, we can indeed be tempted to spend time reading notes and commentaries. It is certainly necessary to understand the literal meaning of the text, but studying the text and reading commentaries should be done at another time: all of this is necessary, but it is a different matter; it nourishes faith in general, but it is not *Lectio*.

84 – Is lingering on what follows or precedes the text another temptation?
Yes, another temptation is precisely the desire to look at what the following or preceding verses say. We must be cautious, as we risk moving from a legitimate search for information to understand the text and place it in context, to a waste of time, which distances us from the goal of *Lectio*. The boundary is minimal and we must be vigilant. The great danger with *Lectio* is to turn it into a text analysis. One still receives light, but it has nothing to do with a word that the living Christ, through His Spirit, communicates to us. *Lectio*, then, is not a study of the text, nor an analysis, but a receptive listening to the Word. In *Lectio*, it is the Lord who speaks to me and gives me His light: the effort of the person lies in listening, receptivity, and thirst.

3- Fruits of *Lectio*

85 – What is one of the first fruits of *Lectio*?
One of the first fruits of *Lectio* is the unification of the day. The loving light that Jesus gives us daily transforms us into a small point, and throughout the day, it is stirred through various

encounters and events, prompting us to activate it with His strength. Every day, therefore, is unified by the grace of *Lectio*, around which thoughts, will, and energies gather, culminating in a small victory with Jesus, allowing Him to become more incarnate in us.

The day will thus resemble a musical variation on the same theme, a single musical phrase: the light received. During the day, other signs will respond, resulting in a concert born from this light. God, as pedagogue, pursues the same idea, but develops it with many nuances. The day, therefore, can often be dedicated to a single theme, a single light. As the days pass, the lights complement each other, and like a puzzle, they slowly compose the entirety of God's mystery.

Keeping a written record of daily *Lectio Divina* is important because it allows us to identify the imprint of divine action, the thread of grace, and the direction in which it moves.

86 – Does the unification of our being also take place?
Yes, if we are perseverant in *Lectio*, day by day, we feel a gradual transformation and unification of the whole person. The two dimensions of the human being (the upper part [intellect that connects with God] and the lower part [will, senses, body]) unify bit by bit, and the two rifts (those between God and the intellect, and between the intellect and the will) slowly disappear. Then, the loving light flows unhindered from the intellect to the acts, bringing a peace and joy that each person can experience.

The two parts of our heart (the upper part [usually given to God] and the lower part [usually occupied by another human being]) also unite around Jesus, thanks to the living relationship we can have with Him during *Lectio*. Each day, He makes us know a new aspect of His profound love, and little by little, our heart is totally conquered by it. This not only does not prevent us from loving others, but allows us to love them with His love!

87 – How is the intellect transformed?
Through *Lectio*, the divine Light of the received Word brings order to the human intellect and restores its original structure; in fact, even more: it teaches it to live with the great mystery of evil. This daily initiation makes the intellect capable of understanding life itself better and discerning the beauty that lies behind unpleasant events. The secret is always the Teacher who is present and teaches His supreme science—the science of salvation, the power of divine love that transforms evil into good: the science of the cross.

The intellect is therefore continually renewed and daily immersed in the Light; the action of the Holy Spirit makes it more subtle and capable of penetrating even the most difficult fields with ever-renewed agility.

88 – Does the perception of the depth of the Bible also grow?
Yes, practising *Lectio* and entering into the understanding of the Scriptures are two things intimately connected. To enter into the understanding of the Scriptures means entering into the cloud of faith, a divine way of reading and listening to the Scriptures. It is about knowing how to penetrate at a level of depth that is entirely different and new.

New dimensions of the text are therefore discovered, new harmonies, new correspondences... the deep unity of the text. This new dimension gives life to the writing; better still, it restores life to it, making it breathe.

Those who practise *Lectio*, while respecting the letter of the text, the secondary author, and their theology, see the word of God as such, above all, deeper, beyond the issues of any individual author.

It should therefore be noted that *Lectio* encourages this deepening, because it does not focus on a text, a thought, or an author, but on God, His word, and His intention, beyond the human author, without causing a short circuit.

It is certain that, by practising *Lectio* daily, those who approach the Bible will have a profound sense, a very insightful and concrete perception, sometimes different from exegesis, yet still recognising its rightful domain.

89- How is the will transformed?

Through the *Lectio*, the will progressively becomes luminous, and little by little, Christ incarnates within it. God's action in us is not superficial; it goes deep, attacking our inner fabric, dissolving it, making it finer, and divinising it. The new man gradually takes over, growing while the old man diminishes. Our will is renewed, piece by piece, recreated every day. Truly, Christ grows in us, slowly takes possession of us, transforms us, directs us: He lives in us.

4- Lectio and the Prayer of the Heart

90- Can *Lectio* be separated from the *Prayer of the Heart*?

No, *Lectio Divina* cannot be separated from the *Prayer of the Heart*, which is the time we give to the Lord to prolong the action of the last Communion we received. This practice is also called Mental Prayer and is similar also to Eucharistic Adoration.

Lectio and the *Prayer of the Heart* are the fundamental pillars of the spiritual life. They represent the prolongation of the two tables of the Mass, which are of equal dignity: that of the Word and that of the Body and Blood of Christ. The one whom we receive in the Eucharist is the same One who spoke to us in His Word. These are the two tables of one Person, who gives Himself in two different ways: one addresses our conscious being, the soul, while the other addresses the spirit, the depths.

Lectio, the prolongation of the table of the Word, nourishes primarily the active part of our being, mainly the intellect and the will; whereas the *Prayer of the Heart*, the prolongation of the table of the Body and Blood of Christ, nourishes primarily the heart or spirit (understood as the highest part of the soul). Both activities are necessary, and the connection between *Lectio* and the *Prayer of the Heart* is the same that unites the table of the Word and the Eucharist.

91- What is the relationship between *Lectio* and the *Prayer of the Heart*?

The two activities, *Lectio* and the *Prayer of the Heart*, have a profound connection and enrich each other. Just as a tree has two parts, the visible part and the roots, so the human being has two realms where his activity takes place: the soul, which is active and can be compared to the visible part of the tree, and the spirit, which is like the deep and passive roots, directly nourished by God in the *Prayer of the Heart*. However, the tree is one, indivisible, and life passes from one part to the other; the tree, by nourishing itself in a different way through these two parts, cannot do without either of them: each one has its own specificity and a different texture. The *Prayer of the Heart* strengthens the will and frees it from many things that would make it enslaved, while *Lectio*, through the gift of self that it evokes each day, continues to open, in the *Prayer of the Heart*, the door to God, so that He may give Himself. Without this, prayer becomes a sterile waiting of a heart that, in reality, remains far from God.

92- Is *Lectio* then the door to the *Prayer of the Heart*?

Yes, the Lord stops at the door of my heart and knocks (cf. Rev 3:20); He wants to enter mystically, that is, through the *Prayer of the Heart*, He wants to enter into me and act in the deepest part of my being. But He puts a condition: He offers me His Word and would like it to incarnate in me. If I listen to it and put it into practice, if I open the door of my will and decide to put His word into practice, then He enters. To open the door of the *Prayer of the Heart*, I must listen to God. It is the effort of the *Lectio* that opens the door to the divine ray of loving contemplation during the *Prayer of the Heart*. Without this effort, God does not (ordinarily) want to enter us through His supernatural action.

Thus, *Lectio* is the door to the *Prayer of the Heart*. On one side, we give ourselves to God in daily life through *Lectio*, and on the other, God gives Himself in the *Prayer of the Heart*. *Lectio*, evoking in us the gift of self, becomes the door to the *Prayer of the Heart*: *"If anyone loves me, he will keep my word, and my Father will love him, and we will come to him and make our home with him."* (John 14:23)

93- Does the *Prayer of the Heart* strengthen and complete the *Lectio*?

Yes, the task of the *Prayer of the Heart* is to shape and inform the will (to give it the form of God), to make it steadfast; it influences the *Lectio* to the extent that it helps the will, in a different way, to be docile to the will of God; it inflames the will greatly. The Holy Spirit clothes the will with love and humility! The Lord, indeed, acts in the *Prayer of the Heart* in a hidden but no less effective way, making the will docile, freeing it from the slavery of sin, adorning it with virtues, and granting it the strength and agility necessary to follow Him. An intense visit from the Lord during the *Prayer of the Heart* enriches the soul with every virtue. This visit is not frequent, but when it happens, it is effective. In a word: the graces received during the *Prayer of the Heart* act in the person and allow them to make great progress in the practice of *Lectio*.

On the other hand, in the *Prayer of the Heart*, God penetrates with His light into the depths of the person, revealing the shadowy areas in a way more powerful and different from *Lectio*; He unveils our hidden potentials. In this sense, the *Prayer of the Heart* clarifies and completes the *Lectio*. One of the main effects of the *Prayer of the Heart* is to make us discover a new and unknown dimension of truth, of our truth. The knowledge of ourselves, of our misery and nothingness, as well as the knowledge that is intimately connected to it—God's mercy—are the two inseparable poles of this deepening that the *Prayer of the Heart* gives to the *Lectio*.

94. Can the *Lectio* extend into the *Prayer of the Heart*?

Since *Lectio* is a supernatural operation, it often happens that the light received allows for a deep recollection, such that after finishing the *Lectio* (which usually lasts about an hour), one feels the need to remain in silence, gathered in God. It must be said clearly: this attitude is excellent, but it is another form of prayer, which we call the *Prayer of the Heart*. It is a more silent way in which the Lord communicates himself in the secrecy of our hearts, just like after Communion during Mass. One feels the need to remain silent, allowing the Lord to act deeply within us. It is excellent and recommended, but it is not the *Lectio* itself. It is useful, in this case, to be aware of this and deliberately set aside time for the *Prayer of the Heart*.

5. The Growth of Spiritual Life

95. What is the starting point of spiritual life?

Baptism is the beginning of spiritual life, the point from which the entire process of our transformation originates. This sacrament immerses us into the Person of Christ and gives us the ability to participate in the life of the Trinity, both consciously and supra-consciously. It is a Seed of Divine Life within us, destined to become a great Tree that bears fruit. However, a seed, when it falls into the ground, can remain there for centuries without sprouting, if it lacks water! Just as the thick outer shell that surrounds the seed cannot open without moisture to allow the Life within to emerge, so too, baptism can remain "buried" for years, even decades, with nothing visibly coming forth from it! Within it lies divine power, but nothing emerges!

Baptism places us in a living and personal relationship with Christ, but this relationship can remain "dormant" within us. We can have a relationship with God similar to that of the Old Testament: a Creator God, powerful, who manages everything but is distant. *Lectio*, however, enables us to enter into a relationship of divine friendship with the Lord, allowing the Seed of Baptism to sprout and begin a process of growth.

96. Where does this process of growth lead?

The path of growth and transformation in following Christ, day after day, leads us to two very important milestones:

1. Union with God (or spiritual marriage), which is reached halfway when the Seed given in Baptism has developed into a mature tree.
2. The Fullness of Divine Charity within us (or the perfection of charity within us), which is attained when the tree begins to bear fruit.

These two goals represent Jesus' plan for each of us: the universal call to holiness. The aim is to grow and reach the fruitfulness that God has destined us for.

97. Is the growth process linear?

No, the growth process is not linear, but divided into stages and involves a fundamental turning point: participation in the Passion, following the Apostles and the authors of the Gospels. This stage is a process of painful regeneration, a crucible that allows us to accept and internalise all the graces contained in the Passion of Christ, so that we can experience His Resurrection, which is the definitive union with Him.

98. Where does all this take place?

This process of "re-creation" occurs in Mary, through the Holy Spirit who dwells and acts in her in fullness. Entered into the womb of Mary, we are nourished, purified, enlightened, and transformed into Christ, until we reach the fullness of His stature and the perfection of Charity (which consists of giving one's life for the salvation of our brothers, as Christ did and with Him).

99. Does spiritual growth happen automatically?

No, it is important to understand that, unlike the child in the mother's womb, we are not totally passive in the action of Mary and the Holy Spirit. We have a role to play! Saint Augustine says that God created us without asking our permission, but He does not save us without our cooperation. In this sense, we are co-authors of our salvation and later of the salvation of our brothers. This is the meaning of our existence on earth. To grow, it is necessary to receive every day the Food that Christ offers us, approaching the two tables of the Mass: the Table of Listening (*Lectio Divina*) and the Table of Immersion in Him (*Prayer of the Heart*). These are the "two legs" to walk toward holiness.

Route of Word in Lectio Divina

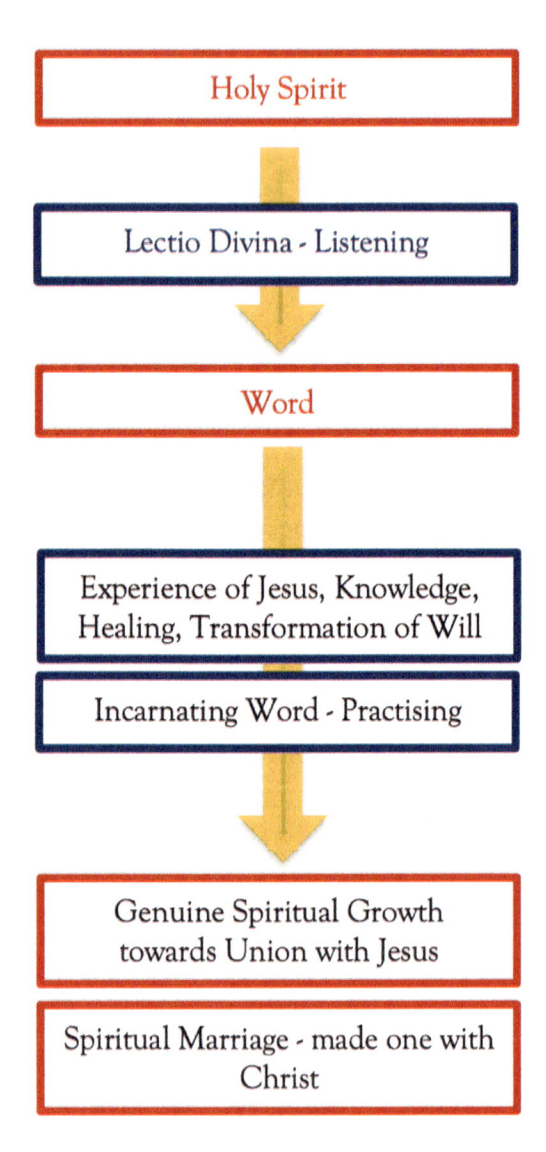

```
┌─────────────────────────┐
│      Holy Spirit        │
└─────────────────────────┘
            ↓
┌─────────────────────────┐
│ Lectio Divina - Listening │
└─────────────────────────┘
            ↓
┌─────────────────────────┐
│          Word           │
└─────────────────────────┘
            ↓
┌─────────────────────────────────┐
│ Experience of Jesus, Knowledge, │
│ Healing, Transformation of Will │
└─────────────────────────────────┘
┌─────────────────────────────────┐
│ Incarnating Word - Practising   │
└─────────────────────────────────┘
            ↓
┌─────────────────────────────────┐
│    Genuine Spiritual Growth     │
│     towards Union with Jesus    │
└─────────────────────────────────┘
┌─────────────────────────────────────┐
│ Spiritual Marriage - made one with  │
│               Christ                │
└─────────────────────────────────────┘
```

Conclusion

100. Is it therefore essential to do *Lectio Divina* every day?
Yes, as we have seen, *Lectio*, and *Lectio* done well, every day, is a powerful means of sanctification. It is the royal way that allows the Lord to truly convert us and to bring about an authentic transformation within us. With *Lectio*, we cover miles in a short time, while, without it, one may be deceived but in reality progresses at a snail's pace: perhaps only a few centimetres over several months. For this reason, we must be attentive to practice it, as it is both a great pillar of spiritual life and a fundamental criterion for evaluating it.

Printed in Great Britain
by Amazon